Amazing Insight...Amazing Profit

Start with very little (under $200) and build a large portfolio of common stock.

Identify the stock to buy using just a few variables.

Know when to sell with one simple calculation.

Learn how to obtain stock without cost.

Obtain dividends from free stock.

Includes the Perfect Stock Buy Method

Information and insight is included about:

Secrets of the professional traders, seasons of the markets, handling market downturns, real estate stocks, mining stocks, low priced stocks, and much more.

Books by Jerry W. Atwood:

The Systems Analyst

STOCK MARKET PROFITS

How to start with a little and end up with a lot

Jerry W. Atwood, PhD

Copyright © 2015 by Jerry W. Atwood
All rights reserved
Published By: Journal of Common Stock
<u>thejournal@jocstock.com</u>
www.jocstock.com

Cover Photos by Carol M. Highsmith

To Gail

Chapter	Title	Page
I	A strong buy	1
II	A dividend strategy	7
III	The Perfect Stock Buy	13
IV	Advice from the Past	24
V	Hotels, Five Cents	28
VI	First Pour	33
VII	Checklist for a Downturn	40
VIII	Change of Season	46
IX	From Top to Bottom	51
X	The Seasonal Method	55
A	Glossary	59
B	The Stock Journal	61

I

How to determine when a stock is a Strong Buy

The following is a brief explanation of how a stock becomes one of our current positions and obtains a rating of Strong Buy. Many investors will suggest that a person is better off trading just a few stocks that they know well rather than have forty of fifty positions which they may not be able to keep up with and may not know as much as they should about each company. We agree, but we also believe that an area of concentration should be determined first and our method is to limit these areas to three or four at a time.

Some investors might pick a sector, such as, energy to concentrate on. Others might pick an industry. We create our own areas. They may or may not be recognized areas, but we usually can target what we are interested in. For example, the recognized industry is Oil

Exploration and Production, but we might just call it Oil and we add a few Bio-Diesel companies and some tar sand companies to compare with the regular oil companies. We obtain these areas by watching the performance of the recognized sectors day by day. The sectors that are up on a regular basis and especially those that are up when the market is down get our attention. We then look within those sectors to find what interest us the most. Information on sector performance is readily available on almost any financial website. We use Business Week, Bloomberg, Google Finance, and Reuters. First, we want to be where the profit is being made.

Second, we want to be in an area where we will be comfortable. For example, we like Ocean Shipping, which is part of the transportation sector, but we would not choose transportation to concentrate on because we would not want to be worrying about airlines, or trucking stocks. We are not attracted to oil tanker companies, but we do like bulk shipping and container shipping. We define what we want and give it a name, in this case we call it Shipping.

An investor or trader should choose three to

four areas to concentrate on and they should be in areas that are of interest. These areas will change but they should not be changed often and without solid reasons.

Once we get our areas of concentration fixed, we then place all of the relevant stocks in a portfolio service and begin the process of finding the common stocks that we want to own for our account and for our client's accounts. These portfolio services are available on most financial websites. We particularly like the one at Morningstar.com.

We are looking for the following:

Current P/E

Forward P/E

Earnings Growth

Debt to Equity

Consensus Estimated Earnings

Price to Book

Return on Assets

Most businessmen will tell you that if they were going to buy a business they would expect a 10% return on the investment. Most business schools teach that to value a business and set a fair price on it; multiply earnings by 10 or use 2 to 3 times book value. We therefore are looking for stocks with less than 10 Forward P/E and less than 3 price/book value. We sort the stocks by Forward P/E and begin the process of comparing all the other values.

First, the Current P/E must be larger than the Forward P/E. That means the company must be going to make more profit in the next 12 months than it made in the last 12 months.

Second, the earnings growth should be positive.

Third, debt to equity should be in line with other companies in the area. Financial companies will have large Debt/Equity, but junior mining companies will have almost no debt.

Fourth, the consensus estimated next years earnings should be roughly equivalent to the Forward P/E. Take the estimated earnings and multiply it by 10. This should be larger than the current price.

Fifth, price to book should be less than 3. The last value is Return on Assets. This is the profit realized for the year divided by total assets. This is sometimes called "the true test of management skill" because management has control of all of the assets, both those bought with shareholder's equity and those bought with borrowed money. At a minimum, more than the current CD rate should be realized. The thinking is that if a company can not make more income than the current CD rate, then there is no reason to run the business at all. Everyone would be better off if the business was closed and all the cash placed into CD's.

We will then sort the portfolio by Forward P/E and beginning at the lowest Forward P/E we look for all of the above values. Remember that our stocks are not from the entire market but only from the areas of concentration we have defined as the best places to be invested at this time. We eliminate any stocks that do not meet the above criteria. We want to end up with about three stocks in each area. We will read the entire file on all these stocks so that we understand the business and what they are

trying to accomplish.

II

A Dividend Strategy

There are many ways to obtain a return on an investment, the most obvious to a great majority of investors is to buy, hold and then sell at a higher price. To others, a smaller group, it is to buy, hold and collect dividends. To the investor seeking income, we recommend a combination of both methods.

Whether to be concerned about dividends at all can be debated. Gerald Loeb, a well known broker and trader, and the author of *The Battle for Investment Survival* has stated that it is futile to try any method other than to strive for large price gains. Loeb called the "income ideas" a self-deception.

Jeremy Siegel, a Professor at the Wharton School, and the author of *Stocks for the Long Run,* says investors are missing out by looking for high growth companies instead of high dividend paying companies. Given enough time high dividend stocks will always outperform high growth stocks. He cites an example of where IBM, one of the greatest growth stocks of all time, was outperformed by Standard Oil (now Exxon-Mobil XOM), a steady stock that paid good dividends. He also notes that his statistics did not include the recent era of high oil prices.

The strategy to take advantage of high dividends is to create a method that not only pays a good income, but also a growing income. Here is a possible method:

1. Select dividend stocks using the same procedure that is presented in the chapter "How to Determine when a Stock is a Strong Buy.". Dividend stocks are usually more expensive than non-dividend paying stocks, so the forward P/E may have to be increased to 12 or 14 to find enough candidates.

2. Seek stocks of companies that have a good chance of increasing in price as well as paying a steady dividend. Seek a reasonable dividend, because companies that have very high dividends are usually in some sort of trouble

and are probably preparing to cut dividends or eliminate them completely.

3. Hold the stock until the price goes up about 20% then sell enough of the stock to return all of your investment including commissions. The stock that is left will continue to pay dividends. The investment that is returned can be placed in another dividend paying stock and the same cycle is repeated. If the stock that is sold is still a good buy, perhaps a few weeks later, then buy the same stock again. (See Below)

4. This is a slow process and must be monitored at least once a month when account statements are available. Quarterly dividend totals should be entered into a column and checked to make sure they are always increasing. Better yet, enter amounts on a graph.

5. Also, if dividends are not withdrawn, then more stock can be bought with the dividends.

To find the stocks that might be considered for investments, a stock screen can be used, perhaps screening for all stocks paying 5% or more dividends. There are lots of places to look. REIT's, Business Investment Companies

(BIC's) and Oil Trusts must pay out most of their earnings to keep a tax-exempt status. Telecommunications, tobacco, and ocean shipping companies have traditionally paid dividends well above any rate that can be obtained from money market accounts or bank accounts.

Here is an actual example of this strategy from our broker's statements. This is how we accumulated 109 shares of Horizon Lines (HRZ) for one of our clients. Horizon was yielding about 8% at this time. Read from the bottom and move up to see the sequence from where we started on 7/17/2008.

Date   Symbol   Description   Commission   Amount
7/27/2009 HRZ   SOLD 78 SHARES OF HRZ AT $5.06   ($7.02) $387.66
6/19/2009 HRZ   BOUGHT 100 SHARES OF HRZ AT $3.8099 ($7.00)   ($387.99)

5/6/2009   HRZ   SOLD 65 SHARES OF HRZ AT $5.77   ($7.01) $368.04
3/27/2009 HRZ   BOUGHT 100 SHARES OF HRZ AT $3.59   ($7.00)   ($366.00)

2/10/2009 HRZ   SOLD 70 SHARES OF HRZ

AT $4.03 ($7.01) $275.09
1/23/2009 HRZ BOUGHT 100 SHARES OF HRZ AT $2.6899 ($7.00) ($275.99)

7/30/2008 HRZ SOLD 20 SHARES OF HRZ AT $11.845 ($7.01) $229.89
7/30/2008 HRZ SOLD 58 SHARES OF HRZ AT $11.83 ($0.01) $686.13
7/17/2008 HRZ BOUGHT 100 SHARES OF HRZ AT $9.0099 ($7.00) ($907.99)

About $18 of dividends were paid during this period.

In summary, we paid $1,937.97 for 400 shares and sold back 291 shares for $1,946.81. Our client then had 109 shares paying 8% dividends at no cost to him. This client has about 4000 shares in his account and 774 of them, as of this writing, were accumulated using this strategy at no cost to the client. This process took about four years and was transacted in a down market most of the time.

This is not a perfect strategy. Gerald Loeb would warn you that if a stock bought for dividends declines in price 30%, it will take many years of collecting dividends to just break even.

This is, of course, why the stocks purchased should be those that meet the strong buy criteria.

III
The Perfect Stock Buy

To perform an analysis so that the end result is the perfect stock buy could turn into a very large project. There would be lots of data to gather and many computer programs to be written. The number of variables that might determine a stock price is probably endless and includes numbers with constantly changing values.

The investor will need a more simple approach.

The perfect stock buy analysis needs only five variables.

1. Price

2. Dividend

3. Projected P/E

4. Market Cap

5. Return on Assets

Here is the data.

Name	Ticker	$ Current Price	% Dividend Yield TTM	Price/ Earnings Forward	$mil Total Assets Latest Qtr	% ROA TTM
Castle Brands Inc	ROX	1.55	0	-151.52	40.95	-25.44
Oi SA ADR	OIBR	2.02	0	-13.39	40,836.79	2.13
Education Management Corp	EDMC	0.3	0	4.29	1,877.04	-35.37
Taseko Mines Ltd	TGB	0.89	0	5.85	829.17	-3.59
Enservco Corp	ENSV	1.76	0	5.87	36.7	12.87
ARMOUR Residential REIT Inc	ARR	3.46	16.81	6.88	17,517.81	-1.15
Chimera Investment Corp	CIM	3.2	11.18	7.15	17,490.97	2.07
Vantage Drilling Co	VTG	0.34	0	8.51	3,603.83	-2.26
TransGlobe Energy Corp	TGA	2.78	5.21	9.02	720.31	8.66
Gerdau SA ADR	GGB	3.39	1.48	14.06	23,286.33	2.72
Halcon Resources Corp	HK	1.34	0	99.01	5,934.41	-23.03
Centrais Eletricas Brasileiras SA ADR	EBR	2.17	0		56,536.61	-4.54
Gafisa SA ADR	GFA	1.44	3.14		2,870.94	10.6
Giordano International Ltd	GRDZF	0.47	9.57		496.96	14.84
Pingtan Marine Enterprise Ltd	PME	2.72	0.76		234.55	58.22
QC Holdings Inc	QCCO	1.7	0		99.02	-14.13

Most brokers will furnish this information, but we use morningstar.com. Here is the latest screen that we are working with:

Name	Ticker	$ Current Price	% Dividend Yield TTM	Price/ Earnings Forward	$mil Total Assets Latest Qtr	% ROA TTM
Castle Brands Inc	ROX	1.55	0	-151.52	40.95	-25.44
Oi SA ADR	OIBR	2.02	0	-13.39	40,836.79	2.13
Education Manage	EDMC	0.3	0	4.29	1,877.04	-35.37
Taseko Mines Ltd	TGB	0.89	0	5.85	829.17	-3.59
Enservco Corp	ENSV	1.76	0	5.87	36.7	12.87
ARMOUR Resident	ARR	3.46	16.81	6.88	17,517.81	-1.15
Chimera Investme	CIM	3.2	11.18	7.15	17,490.97	2.07
Vantage Drilling C	VTG	0.34	0	8.51	3,603.83	-2.26
TransGlobe Energ	TGA	2.78	5.21	9.02	720.31	8.66
Gerdau SA ADR	GGB	3.39	1.48	14.06	23,286.33	2.72
Halcon Resources	HK	1.34	0	99.01	5,934.41	-23.03
Centrais Eletricas	EBR	2.17	0		56,536.61	-4.54
Gafisa SA ADR	GFA	1.44	3.14		2,870.94	10.6
Giordano Internati	GRDZF	0.47	9.57		496.96	14.84
Pingtan Marine En	PME	2.72	0.76		234.55	58.22
QC Holdings Inc	QCCO	1.7	0		99.02	-14.13

Here is the criteria that is used for the perfect stock buy.

Price. To keep the risk manageable and to have enough cash to make at least six buys, the price of the stock should be between 1 and 3. When the market is at record levels as it has been lately, the best place to look is in foreign stocks.

.10 >>>>>>>>>>>>>>>>>>>>>>>>>>>>>>>>>>>>>3.99
_____

At this price level even a small percentage change will create enough profit to sell and keep some free shares.

Dividends. We will prefer dividend paying stocks. A good rate to look for is at least six percent, but lower dividends will work if the other criteria is good. If a stock does not pay dividends but it seems to be a strong buy it might be considered for the portfolio but not as part of the Perfect Buy method.

Projected P/E. This is the price to earnings ratio based on the projected earnings. Projected earnings are developed by security analysts which work for large brokerage firms, mutual funds, and retirement funds. The number produced is not a sure thing, it is an estimate but it is produced by some of the best people in the market, many who have Master degrees in finance. It is knowing the projected P/E that gives the Perfect Buy Method investor an edge over the average investor. It is not perfect but it is better than anything the individual investor could produce without much time and effort.

The projected P/E should be less than 10. Values of 3, 4, and 5 are ideal for the perfect stock buy.

Market Cap. This is the current price of the stock multiplied by the number of shares outstanding. There is a lot of flexibility in this criteria but it is best to look for at least one billion in market cap.

Return on Assets. This is the profit for a year divided by the total assets on the books, except for intangibles. If this figure is negative then there has been a loss. It is best to pass on any stocks with negative ROA unless other information is very compelling.

Here are the steps needed in this method.

1. Use a stock screen to find possible stocks to buy. Start with price and dividends.

2. Enter these stocks into a portfolio that contains the criteria presented above.

3. Sort the list by lowest projected P/E. Delete any stocks with negative projected P/E.

4. Buy 100 shares each of the two or three stocks with the lowest projected P/E.

5. Monitor the price of the stock. The objective is to get all the investment back and keep 30 shares of the stock at no cost. Divide the total investment in the stock by 70. This will give the price the stock must reach to accomplish the objective. It is best to try to buy 300 shares and sell 200 so that there will be 100 free shares. In this case, divide the total investment by 200 and that will give the price to sell.

Check the Return on Assets (ROA) and eliminate the stocks with negative returns.

List Analysis

Let us examine what we have in this list and see what stocks we would buy, if any. The forward P/E is sorted low to high. Notice that ROX and OIBR are negative so we will eliminate them.

EDMC and TGB have projected earnings that meet the criteria but they show negative ROA.

We certainly want to keep them on the list, but we would not buy them right now.

ENSV is the first stock that meets all the criteria, but it has a very small market cap. We will put it on the buy list, but we might change it if better stocks are available.

ARR and VTG have negative ROA and we will pass on them. CIM has very low ROA and although it meets all of our criteria we will wait on better ROA figures.

TGA meets all the criteria and will be on the buy list. It would be better if the projected P/E was lower, but it is below 10.

GGB and HK are above the requirement that the P/E should be below 10 and will not be considered.

The rest of stocks on this list are without any projected earnings and will not be considered at this time, however there may be some very good buys here. It depends upon how much research the investor wants to do.

We have ended up with two stocks we should buy, ENSV and TGA.

Perfect Stock Buy Reality

Some would say that nothing works in real life the same way it works on paper or in theory. Here are some actual trades that were done using the Perfect Stock method. All of these are on our broker's statements and all are trades made using the same method as stated above.

2/10/2014 EBR   BOUGHT 100 SHARES OF EBR AT $2.1299 ($219.99)
4/9/2014 EBR   SOLD 65 SHARES OF EBR AT $3.3201 $208.80

2/10/2014 TGS   BOUGHT 100 SHARES OF TGS AT $1.8797 ($194.97)
5/9/2014 TGS   SOLD 70 SHARES OF TGS AT $2.7601 $186.20

7/24/2014 ROX   BOUGHT 300 SHARES OF ROX AT $0.8583 ($265.78)
10/6/2014 ROX   SOLD 200 SHARES OF ROX AT $1.29 $250.99

3/21/2014 ROX   BOUGHT 100 SHARES OF ROX AT $1.2891   ($135.91)

10/28/2014 ROX SOLD 80 SHARES OF ROX AT $1.7201 $130.60

11/27/2013 QCCO BOUGHT 100 SHARES OF QCCO AT $1.8399 ($190.99)
2/7/2014 QCCO SOLD 75 SHARES OF QCCO AT $2.58 $186.49

11/5/2012 BSI BOUGHT 100 SHARES OF BSI AT $2.6599 ($272.99)
5/2/2013 BSI SOLD 65 SHARES OF BSI AT $3.74 $236.09

The most obvious difference in the theory and the reality is that the buy amounts and the sell amounts are not the same. This will be true of most transactions. Low price stocks can change by .05 or more from the time the sell trade is entered to the time the trade is executed. Also, the spread my be larger between the bid and the ask. The trades above were made at a time that the market was making record highs and many traders were concerned that the market could go down any minute so these stocks were sold probably too quickly to avoid getting caught in a downturn.

The trades above cost a total of $1,280.63 and when sold realized $1,199.17. We kept 225 shares at a cost of $81.46 or 36 cents per share. The shares are not completely free, but we will continue to call them free because that is the objective of the trade and if the investor has the patience to wait until the sell point is reached they will be free.

In many cases, the amount received for the shares that are sold will be greater than the amount paid for the initial shares. It is like being paid to take the free shares.

Summary

These steps can be repeated over and over to build a stock account containing thousands of shares that cost nothing. However, this is not just a mechanical action, some monitoring will be needed as the market changes.

IV
Advice from the Past

The active investor will most likely admit that they know much more about what to do with their money than they did when they first started investing. Therefore, it would be wise to pay attention to investors who have been extremely successful and have many years of experience and have written about what they have learned.

The following short notes are advice from those that have invested in the stock market for many years and have not only been successful but have become legends on Wall Street.

Gerald Loeb

During his career he was known as the "Dean of Wall Street". He wrote a classic book entitled *The Battle for Investment Survival* and here is his advice:

1. Buy only the active listed stocks.

2. Do not borrow money to invest and do not use margin accounts.

3. Invest in and monitor only five stocks at a time.

4. Investment is a very inexact science.

5. Do not be 100% invested.

Benjamin Graham

Known to most investors as the greatest investment adviser of all time. Graham wrote a book called *The Intelligent Investor.*

Thousands of successful investors have stated that this book had the greatest influence on their careers. Warren Buffet has stated that he follows Graham's teachings in making his investments. Here are a few of Graham's ideas:

1. Every listed stock has a price at which it would be a good buy and another price at which it should be sold. It is the challenge to the stock investor to know these prices.

2. Try to buy at a price that is not more than the net asset value of the stock.

3. Buy the stock of large companies with a good record of paying dividends.

4. Do not pay more than 15 P/E.

William J. O'Neil

O'Neil is the founder of the Investor's Business Daily and has thousands of followers of his investment methods. His book *How to Make Money in Stocks* sold over a million copies. He is also a follower of Gerald Loeb's ideas.

1. Cut Losses. If stock price goes down 8%, sell it.

2. Have a set of buying and selling rules.

3. Try to select companies that are number one in their market.

4. Select stocks which have return on equity of 17% or greater.

V
Hotels, Five Cents

If an investor looked at a sheet of numbers for commercial real estate, on March 9, 2009, the investor would see in the column for Price/Book:

hotels, 5 cents on the dollar.

home builders, 4 cents.

shopping centers, 7 cents.

office buildings, 15 cents.

apartment complexes, 14 cents.

warehouses, 11 cents.

This is what it would cost you to buy one dollar of the book value of these companies. (Book Value is Assets minus Liabilities, but intangible assets, such as, goodwill, are not counted.)

We are not stating that you should start buying commercial real estate, but with valuations like these it is time to put real estate companies on the watch list.

Here are the companies that the valuation data above came from: (These are not buy recommendations, the possible buys are at the end of this chapter).

hotels, 5 cents, Interstate Hotels (IHRI).

home builders, 4 cents, Beazer Homes (BZH).

shopping centers, 7 cents, General Growth (GGP).

office buildings, 15 cents, S L Green (SLG).

apartment complexes, 14 cents, Colonial Properties (CLP).

warehouses, 11 cents, First Industrial (FR).

Commercial real estate has always had its up and down cycles and real estate cycles can be quite long. When the savings and loan crisis of the late 80's began and when the government formed the Resolution Trust Corporation (RTC) many pieces of real estate were sold for 50% of value, but nothing like some of the values listed above. Most real estate professionals believe it will be at least seven years before commercial real estate begins to get back to normal and that depends upon when the credit markets get back to normal.

Most investors do not even want to hear the word "real estate" because they believe it was the real estate mania of 2005 and 2006, along with the financing of that mania, that was the cause of the recession. However, real estate is an asset similar to gold. Its value may go up and down, but it will not become worthless; as a piece of paper or a business model can become when a recession begins.

As common stock investors or traders what should we do about stock in real estate companies? The situation seems almost classic in the sense that it is a contrary situation, it fits many of the old sayings "buy when blood is running in the streets", "buy, when everyone else is selling," but we do not suggest that you buy or even hold.

Here is what the professional real estate investors suggest. There is a direct proven correlation between hotels and the health of the real estate industry. The Revenue Per Available Room (Rev Par) is directly tied to consumer and business sentiment. If Rev Par is down, the consumer is not confident in taking holidays and spending on vacations, and businessmen are holding back on travel as much as they can. Rev Par is expected to be down about 7% this year when compared to last year. When Rev Par gets even, that is, when this quarter's Rev Par is equal to the same quarter's Rev Par of last year then that is the bottom of the Hotel cycle and signals the bottom of the entire real estate cycle. Rev Par would be 0%, or a small increase. This has been true of the last three real estate cycles.

In the meantime, those that can not wait to take advantage of some real estate stock investments, we have checked the numbers in our data base of 100 real estate public companies. None of these companies can be considered Strong Buys, mostly because earnings are trending down instead of up, and rising earnings are one of the requirements of a Strong Buy. However, there are two stocks worth considering:

IRS   IRSA Investments.

WRI   Weingarten Realty.

IRS is an Argentine real estate company with land holdings and interest in banks, hotels and shopping centers. There is only one analyst that covers the company but they have estimated earnings will go from .32 a share to 2.78. IRS sells for 45 cents of book and revenue has been growing at a 46% a year rate.

WRI owns over 300 shopping centers mostly in the Southwest U. S. There are three analyst that cover the company and the consensus is that earnings will rise from .51 to 1.32 a share. It sells for 59 cents of book. In normal times, WRI would be a $40.00 stock, but it is selling now for about $10.00. We believe IRSA will rise to $24.00 a share as the economy improves and WRI will get to $15.00.

They are both worth putting on a watch list but are not yet Strong Buys. Remember, when Rev Par is 0% when compared to last year, that is the time to buy. As long as Rev Par is negative compared to last year, it is too soon to buy.

If you are going to buy some real estate stocks because they are so cheap, consider that when we were putting this book together about three weeks ago it was called, "Hotels, 9 cents". Since then the price to book of IHR has dropped to where we now call it "Hotels, 5 cents".

VI

First Pour – A Road to Mining Profits

The big problem in trying to determine which small cap, speculative mining stocks to buy is that there is almost no fundamental data available. There will usually be no significant earnings, no analyst that follow the companies, no estimated income, no P/E, no ROA, no Debt to Equity Ratio, no Price to Book Ratio and unless you want to do a lot of work you may not even find a description of the company or its business objectives.

It is certainly enough to make most investors want to stay away from small company mining stocks, especially start ups. However, the other side of this problem is that tremendous profits can be made and much significant wealth created by investing in mining stocks. There are also many followers of mining stocks that will state that if you just pick one out of ten small mining companies that develops a large gold, silver, copper or any other kind of mining business it will more than make up for the nine that that fold up and go away.

Before we state one possible solution to investing in mining stocks, it will be easier to understand this solution if the development of a mining company is presented in the most basic terms. Here is a mining company:

1. Exploring. A company has been formed and is going to attempt to locate mineral deposits that can be extracted economically. This is the time that there is very little information that an investor can use to base a decision to buy the stock. Almost all Profit and Loss Statements will show losses because the company has no revenue and is spending large amounts for land leases, personnel, equipment, fuel, etc.

2. Extracting. If something is located and geologists and mining engineers agree that it can be mined with a profit, the company will bring in equipment and miners and begin to produce whatever they have located. This can be rough ore or if they have a mill it will be some type of concentrate. This is the time that revenue will be coming in and the Profit and Loss Statement may begin to show profit instead of a loss.

3. Producing. If all of this is successful and maybe a few more mines have been developed, after a few years the company will no longer be considered a speculative mining company. Investors will have all the information they need to make an informed and intelligent decision to purchase or not purchase the stock.

Here is the mining company in a graphical form:

exploring   extracting   producing

>>>

Right at the end of the word "Extracting" at the "g" is where the company changes from no revenue to having revenue. In silver mining this is called "First Pour", that is, the first silver that is obtained from the mine is melted and poured into a silver bar. In gold mining, this is called a "Dore". In copper mining this is called "Concentrate".

Those investors who have been trading in mining stocks for many years, almost all of them that have been successful have purchased stocks in the producing area because that is where they could get evaluation data. We once had a rule that we would "buy no stock priced under a dollar." However, a closer look at mining companies that had finished exploring and were beginning to produce, made us cancel this rule. But we had no hard evidence that this was a good decision.

An experiment was set up. It is listed in steps, so if other investors want to evaluate this method, they can follow the same steps:

A. In a search engine (we used Google), we put in the words "2009 First Pour". It is important to put in the current year or the search engine will give "First Pours" from four or five years ago.

B. On August 6, 2009 we assembled this list from our search:

Stock	Ticker	Price Aug 6th
Atna	ATNAF	.66
ECU Silver	ECUXF	.44
Timmins	TMGOF	.45
CGA Mining	CGAFF	1.44
Apollo	AGT	.45
Avocet	AVVGF	1.12

| Etruscan | ETRUF | .21 |

C. On November 5, 2009, approximately three months later, we found the prices for these stocks and listed the price increase or the decrease. We added the S & P 500 for comparison.

Stock	Ticker	Price Aug 6	Price Nov 5	Change
Atna	ATNAF	.66	.71	+7%
ECU Silver	ECUXF	.44	.76	+55%
Timmins	TMGOF	.45	.95	+111%
CGA Mining	CGAFF	1.44	1.59	+10%

Apollo	AGT	.45	.54	+20%
Avocet	AVVGF	1.12	1.28	+14%
Etruscan	ETRUF	.21	.50	+138%
S and P 500	SPY	999	1065	+6.6%

Average increase   +50.7%

At first glance, it seems that the experiment was a success. All of the seven stocks beat the S & P 500 increase and all of them were profitable in the short span of three months.

However, there is a need to purchase these stocks in the thousands instead of the hundreds. For example, a trader who bought a 100 shares of ETRUF (the stock with the most increase in price) would have spent $21.00 and would have had $50.00 in three months. This is a true 138% increase, but it is also only $29.00. Take away $14.00 for brokers commission and the trader has $15.00, which is not much for all this work. Do some calculations on buying 5,000 shares or 10,000 shares and it will be clear that with speculative mining stocks the investor must think "thousands" not "hundreds". Also, there is a need to buy the entire list if you are going to obtain the benefit of the average increase. If the investor had bought just ATNAF, there would only be a 7% increase in the stock.

In summary, the experiment has convinced us that there is a valid strategy in timing purchases of stock in mining companies at the time the company is moving from explorer to producer. We will be obtaining some more lists and purchasing that entire list in the near future. It is also possible that we might try a search on "first gold Dore", "first copper concentrate" and how about "first oil well".

VII

Checklist for a Downturn

There are many quotes about the Stock Market but probably the most true is "Stocks will go up and Stocks will go down". Another that applies today is "Nothing (Stocks or Market) will go up forever".

If an investor is going to prepare for a downturn in the market then it would be wise to know when there is a downturn. Many stock investors use the 52 week highs and lows. If there are more stocks making highs than lows then the market is moving up. If more stocks are making lows then that is a signal that the market is in a downturn.

In this book we use the 100 day moving average and the 200 day moving average to verify the market is in a downturn. These are easily obtained from any chart at a brokerage website or a financial website.

At the website www.google.com/finance anyone

can type in SPY, click on at least a six month view, then at the bottom of the chart click Technical and then request the simple moving average (SMA) and finally type 100 in the box for Period.

The S and P 500 index (SPY) crossed down over the 100 day moving average on January 29, 2010. This is not the end of the market, but it is a time to be more cautious and less speculative. Sometimes the market will move back up almost immediately and the downturn signal will be over. Sometimes the market will move down and up, crossing the 100 day moving average so many times that many investors will get tired of keeping up with it. Please do not take this lightly because great damage can be done to portfolios if these signals are ignored.

Just as there is a method for buying (see Chapter 1) there is also a method for a market downturn.

Here is what we do and we have found that it works for us. The main objective is preservation of capital because when the market changes the investor will want to have cash to buy new bargains made available by the downturn.

Checklist for 100 day moving average (the SPY is below its 100 day moving average):

1. _____Take profit in all positions where there is even the smallest profit. Turn all of this investment and the profit into cash.

2. _____Quit Buying into new positions.

3. _____Get rid of Margin. Sell enough so that there is no margin used in your account. Better yet, contact your broker and take the margin feature off of your account.

4._____Do not sell short or buy any ETF's that are short. The investor that is short is in the same position as they were in before they sold short, because they do not know when the market will move back up. (See Market neutral at the end of this chapter)

Checklist for 200 day moving average (the SPY is below its 200 day moving average):

Let us hope that we do not need this checklist.

1._____Clean house. Look at every position in the portfolio. Sell every position that is marginal. That is, we will keep only those that have great fundamentals and that we really believe in. We will strive to have as much cash as possible.

2. _____Do not use options. Many investors will want to buy puts to protect the position. This ties up cash and it is like saying "I know when the market will turn". No one really knows when the market will turn. Many investors believe that selling covered calls will give them some income during the down turn, but a call will only protect for a few points. What sense does it make to obtain $300 for a call when the stock has lost $2000?

3. _____Wait for the upturn. If you sense a turnaround in the market, perhaps the SPY has crossed the 200 day moving average on its way up, then some buying is appropriate. Buy with caution and only buy those stocks with the best fundamentals.

Most downturns will last only a few weeks or less. There is no reason to believe that this is the start of a bear market. Historically, bear markets only start when there is a rise in interest rates and that has probably not happened.

If an investor wants to stay active there is an exception to the rule "Do not short" and the rule "wait for the upturn" and that is to be Market Neutral. This means you have a short position and a long position in similar items at approximately the same price. We are going to buy the SPY and buy the PSQ. The SPY will put us long on the largest and strongest 500 companies. The PSQ will put us short the 100 stocks that make up the NASDAQ index. The theory is that the NASDAQ stock prices will decrease more than the S and P 500 stocks.

If an investor is in this position, there is no need to be concerned about the market. The only objective is to have the "spread" or the difference widen in our favor. Because the price of these ETF's are not equal we will approximately even them out by buying two PSQ's for each share of SPY.

Remember that this is only for the event that the SPY drops below the 200 day moving average.

In summary, there are almost no actions that will be profitable during a market downturn. It is a time for waiting, and accumulating as much cash as possible to use when the market turns. If an investor must have an activity (some action) then look into commodities or the commodity ETF's. Jim Rogers, the author of the book *Hot Commodities*, stated that: "Historically, there has been a negative correlation between the price movement of stocks and commodities. On any chart of bull markets in stocks and commodities, they are parallel lines going in separate directions." He further notes that this data has been true all the way back to 1871.

Remember that this is only for the event that the SPY drops below the 200 day moving average.

It will be great if we never need any of the information in this article, but someday we will. Copy this and keep it in a safe place.

VII

Change of Season, Change of Trend

Today, June 21, is the first day of summer. The corn and the soybeans have been planted, to grow, and then to be harvested in the fall. A definite seasonal trend. Most of us did not like the snow, ice and cold air of the winter, but now it is mostly forgotten so we can now complain about the heat of the summer. A definite seasonal trend.

Is there a seasonal trend in the stock markets? There seems to be several trends that an investor should know about. The worst month in the market is September, although October probably has the worst reputation because of the many market crashes recorded in October. But October is a positive month, maybe it is because the market is brought down so much by September, it has nowhere to go but up by October. The only other month that is negative is February, but the average downturn is so small that it can be disregarded.

By historical records we have ten months to trade that will be positive and only two months that will be negative. A definite seasonal trend and a good one for those that are buying and selling common stocks.

But, of course, stocks are not like corn or soybeans and will not have a "time to plant, and a time to reap." Maybe the seasons of the market are just developed tradition. That is, a couple of bad years in September made traders avoid September in the future. No one can exactly explain why the seasonal trend exists, but it is statistical fact that it does exist.

This first chart is a general overview of the seasons of the market.

Date	Explanation	Trend
November 1	This is the beginning of the market. Almost the same as planting corn and soybeans in the middle of May.	Up
May 15	A time to be out of the	Down

	market.	
June 15	Market will be O. K. until August, but there will be one or two dips that will be overcome by August 10th.	Up
August 10	This is a time to be completely out of stocks.	Down
October 20	Begin to analyze the stocks that will be bought, beginning November 1st.	Up

The investor should believe in the fundamentals of individual stocks much more than believing in chart patterns, or seasons, or any kind of market timing; however, the investor should also believe in the old saying, "Don't Fight the Trend".

This next chart is what we are going to do with a couple of selected accounts. The S and P 500 is blank and that is where we will record the outcome of following the market seasons. This will be reported (after we have tried this approach) on the first day of summer.

Date	Explanation	Trend	S a n

			d P 500
June 21	Buy stocks. Buy carefully and begin to sell off August 1st.	Up	
August 10	Take a vacation. Hold only the stocks that we are sure we can not live without.	Down	-
October 20	Begin to analyze new stock positions.	Up	-
November 1	Buy stocks. Stay active through April, but because of what happened in prior years, get out before May 1st.	Up	-
May 1	Take a vacation. Get ready for the first day of summer.	Down	

We realize that everyone has there own method of buying and selling common stock and we are not suggesting that you follow this chart or the seasons that are represented. This is an experiment, not a proven method. Copy this page and follow along with us by filling in the S and P 500 blanks.

There are many places to get more information. We recommend Ron Insana's book *Trend Watching*, which has a complete history of the markets.

Gerald Loeb the author of *The Battle for Investment Survival* probably had the closest idea to a proven method when he stated:

Take a position, and if the trend is wrong, get out. If the trend is correct, buy more.

From Top to Bottom

This chapter is being written at the very bottom (so far) of the stock market. The market can go lower, but it is doubtful it will because we are entering the time of the traditional summer rally. We may have less in our accounts, but we also have more bargain stocks to chose from.

If an investor is experienced and has been in the market for a while, all of this article will be familiar. If an investor just started in the market at the top of the market (so far), then here is some information that we hope will be helpful in understanding what has happened to your stock account (what's left of it).

The common stock market is a cycle that no one can predict. On one extreme, some believe we are headed for another "great depression" which will be worse than the one of the 30's. On the other extreme, some believe we are just pausing while the world economy begins to generate transactions which will make anyone who is willing to buy stock, wealthy beyond their dreams.

In a graphic form, here is what the top and the bottom look like:

Market	Characteristic	How to Recognize	Act
Top	Stocks are selling at very high Price to Earnings ratios and Price/Book ratios. Business conditions are generally good. Lots of new highs everyday and very few new lows.	Everyone is enthused about the stock market and it is the topic of conversation everywhere. The mailman and the bartender are giving out stock tips.	Sell
Bottom	Stocks are selling at very low Price to Earnings ratios and stock prices are at bargain prices but few investors want to buy and the public has no money.	Most people do not want to talk about stocks. There is fear about running short of income, losing a job, paying the rent and all things financial.	Buy

If we, as investors or traders, look at our portfolios after two months of turmoil and now six days of down markets we might be inclined to get out of the market or we might be considering that the stock market is just not for us. However, remember that Warren Buffet had the viewpoint, "Buy when others are fearful, and sell when others are greedy." Maybe the most famous old saying is from Baron Rothschild who said, "Buy when the blood is running in the street". This was also emphasized by Sir John Templeton, one of the most famous investors of all time.

It is time to find the bargains, but if an account is full of purchases of stocks that can only be sold at a large loss and has little cash, you have what is called a "frozen" account. All of your holdings are waiting for the market to come back up, but there is no cash to buy any of the bargains that are available from the downturn.

When you spot a bargain that you would like to take advantage of, try to find a position that you hold that is about the same value and sell it and then buy the new bargain. An investor is simply evaluating whether they would rather hold the new stock on the way up instead of the old stock that was sold at a loss. This method does not change the value of the account.

The investor should see a global economy where over seven billion people have to be fed, clothed, housed, transported and financed. There is little possibility that the investors who provide these needs will not be rewarded. When we watch those who are selling stocks and not seeing the possibilities of the future economy we believe we are looking at the investors who love to be fully invested as the market is on the upturn and then want to sell out at the bottom. This, of course, is the opposite of what should be done.

Here is some advice from some of the greatest investors:

Compare what you own with what is available.

...Gerald Loeb

Market Cycles give the investor a chance to buy at good prices and sell at good prices...Benjamin Graham

However you view it, we are going to be in the summer upturn soon. Everything will be fine.

Just start selling before September.

The Seasonal Method Experiment

Today, June 21, is the first day of summer. One year ago we wrote the following:

Today, June 21, 2010, is the first day of summer. The corn and the soybeans have been planted, to grow, and then to be harvested in the fall. A definite seasonal trend. Most of us did not like the snow, ice and cold air of the winter, but now it is mostly forgotten so we can now complain about the heat of the summer. A definite seasonal trend.

Then a question was asked. Were there seasonal trends to the stock market? Could they be traded?

In the chapter Change of Season, we presented a table that projected the seasonal trends of the market. Then we proposed that we would check these trends for the next year. Here is the table we presented:

Date	Explanation	Trend	S and P 500
June 21	Buy stocks. Buy carefully and begin to sell off August 1st.	Up	1117
August 10	Take a vacation. Hold only the stocks that we are sure we can not live without.	Down	-
10/20/15	Begin to analyze new stock positions.	Up	-
11/01/15	Buy the stocks on the Strong Buy list. Stay active through April, but because of what happened this year, get out before May 1st.	Up	-
May 1	Take a vacation. Get ready for the first day of summer.	Down	-

To be able to check the results and to see if this method is viable, we will buy ten shares of the SPY, which is the ETF for the S and P 500 index. Therefore, we are starting with $1,117.00 invested in the SPY.

Results from June 21, 2010 to June 20, 2011

June 21 - Our table states that the trend is up and will hold until August 10. At that time we are at 1121 and we are up, but not much. We will sell and if we were counting commission we would be down $10.

August 10 - Our table states that the trend is down and will hold until October 20. Since the trend is down we will sell and stay out of the SPY. On October 20 we are at 1178 and we have missed $57 in profit. The trend was not down.

November 1 - Our table states that the trend is up and will hold until May 1. We will buy back in at 1184 and we will have $1,184.00 invested in the SPY. On May 1 the S and P 500 is at 1361, the trend was up.

May 1 - Our table states that we should take a vacation, so we will sell and have $1,361.00. This is a profit of $177 and a return of 15%. Please note that the trend for May 1 is down and the S and P 500 has dropped from 1361 to 1295 as of June 21, 2011.

Conclusions:

1. It would be difficult to make much profit on these trends except for the November to May trend and the downturn on May 1 to June 21. These two trends seem to be well established

and occur every year with a few exceptions.

2. It is probably better to let the trends guide us as to when to be aggressive and when to pull back.

3. In the future, the investor should be fully invested from November to May and will hold off on new purchases from May 1 to June 21.

Appendix A

Glossary

Current P/E: The price of the stock divided by the earnings. If a stock sells for $15.00 and earns $1.00 a share then the P/E is 15. This is based on earnings that have been made. There is no way of knowing if the company will make this amount of earnings in the future.

Forward P/E: This is the price to earnings ratio based on the projected earnings. Projected earnings are developed by security analysts which work for large brokerage firms, mutual funds, and retirement funds. The number produced is not a sure thing, it is an estimate but it is produced by some of the best people in the market, many who have Master degrees in finance.

Earnings Growth: Current earnings compared to last years earnings or to some average of past earnings.

Debt to Equity: The total debt compared to

equity. A figure of 2 means the company has twice the debt than it has funds from investors. A figure of 0 means the company has no debt. The Debt to Equity figure should be in line with other companies in the area. Financial companies will have large Debt/Equity, but junior mining companies will have almost no debt.

Consensus Estimated Earnings: This is the average of all the estimates from all the analysts who follow the company.

Price to Book: The book value is all the assets minus the liabilities. The price per share compared to the book value per share will tell the investor what he is getting for his money.

Return on Assets: This is what the company earns on all the assets of the company expressed as a percentage of total assets. This depicts what management can accomplish with both equity and borrowed funds.

Appendix B

The Stock Journal

Every investor should keep a journal of market conditions, stocks that are being analyzed, trends that are noticed and anything that might be a factor in buying and selling stocks. Review of this journal will be helpful in understanding what is being done right and what is being done wrong.

Here is an example of a journal that was kept from about the time of the market downturn in 2008-2009 until 2015.

Journal Entries

January 12, 2015

In past years we would be entering into the Journal that this is the best time to be buying stock, but this year is not like past years. With market indexes at record levels and more budget talks and debt ceiling talks coming in a few months, we will stick with these stocks until April 2015.

Strong Buys

Stocks

2015

Name	Ticker	Price	Yield
Whiting USA	WHX	1.80	122%
Trans Global	TGA	3.28	4.2%
QC Holdings	QCCO	1.90	0
Armour Res.	ARR	3.57	16.4%
Box Ships	TEU	.83	0

| Vale SA | VALE | 8.55 | 6.6% |

**Journal Entries
November 2, 2013**

In past years we would be entering into the Journal that this is the best time to be buying stock, but this year is not like past years. With market indexes at record levels and more budget talks and debt ceiling talks coming in a few months, we will stick with dividend stocks until March 2014.

April 15, 2013

We are selling all stocks that do not pay a dividend of at least 6%. This is not because of the current market decline but because May is only a few weeks away. No one knows if the market will follow its traditional May decline, but we have been right many more times than wrong by believing this.

We are posting a new list of stocks for the summer.

October 14, 2012

We are starting to buy and we are staying with the dividend stocks for a while. The Strong Buy list should be good until April.

May 4, 2012

This is May, a time when most markets will decline. We have sold all stocks except for the strong Buys. For more information on this strategy, see our article Change of Season.

We taking SSN Samson off the Strong Buy list and replacing it with PBR Petrobras.

We are adding a Strong Buy Dividend Stocks list, which we will use during the summer downturn.

April 3, 2012

The S and P 500 was up 12% in the first quarter. We have had a good market.

We are now starting to sell all stocks in the account and will continue to do so until we have changed the account to dividend stocks. We are getting close to May. Sometime in October we will begin to buy again.

February 1, 2012

The market is up about 5% since the first of the year. We expect more upward movement through April.

We are taking PostRock off the Strong Buy list. Estimated earnings have been cut way back and it no longer qualifies as a Strong Buy. We are adding Navios Maritime which qualifies and also has a 6.5% dividend.

January 2, 2012

Beginning in 2012, we are reporting the top Strong Buys without regard to the concentration.

We expect a good market until the end of April. We will sell or at least lighten up positions on May 1, 2012.

October 18, 2011

It seems that the bottom of this market will be October 4, 2011. Now is the time to be looking for the bargain stocks and to begin to buy. We will be buying from the Strong Buy List and from the High Risk page.

October 1, 2011

We are dropping Tech as a group and adding Agriculture. This group will include fertilizers, food producers, machinery, and farm operations. The Tech stocks listed are still Strong Buys so we will leave them up for a while, but we will not be adding anymore.

September 2, 2011

There are a lot of bargains in the market right now, but it is impossible to know if now is the time to buy them. We are waiting until October 15th, when the market will begin to recover. September is the worst month of the year for common stocks. Here is an article from the Financial Post which explains more: Seasonal Influences.

August 5, 2011

It is a time to hold and wait. In the history of the markets, a large downturn or panic selling

does not define the bottom. The turning point will come several months later. For more information see our article From Top to Bottom.
July 13, 2011

Advance America (AEA) has reached the target price and is being sold today. AEA price has more than doubled since we posted it as a Strong Buy. It is being replaced by a similar company with the same fundamentals as AEA. QCCO is also known as "Quick Cash".
July 1, 2011

The downturn seems to be over as the market has been up five days in a row and is back above the 100 day moving average on the S and P 500. We are going to start buying. Every investor has their own favorite industry to trade in, but we are going to stick with shipping. DRYS has been upgraded by Goldman Sachs and many of the ocean shipping stocks are trading below book value. ONAV is priced at 4 cents on the dollar.
June 3, 2011

The last time this entry appeared was May 19, 2010. We are posting it again as it appeared then.

The S and P 500 index has crossed below the 100 day moving average of 1317. It is time to implement a plan for a market downturn. If you do not have one, feel free to use ours which is at Checklist for a Downturn.

This downturn may only last a few days, or it may last for several months. What ever your plan or method is, "do something". Do not stand by and let the value of your portfolio shrink by 3 to 4 percent per day.
May 2, 2011

We have had a good November to May market which has followed the historical trend of other years, however, we are entering May which is a time that most commodity prices begin to decline and this decline usually takes the stocks down with them. If a trader or an investor wishes to continue on as normal, then there is a chance that there will be no change in the market and it will continue upward. Please watch the S and P 500 and if it declines to 1300 that is the first signal that the market is turning down.

Smart Modular (SMOD) has agreed to be purchased by Silver Lake Partners for $9.25 a

share. This is a good profit from $5.96 when we first listed it as a Strong Buy.
April 2, 2011

This is the time of year when ocean shipping begins to pick up and the stocks revive along with the increase in business. We will not buy just because a company is in the shipping business. Some of them still have big problems from the recession. We will buy only DRYS, SB, and NM which have good financials and qualify as Strong Buys. Seanergy is still on the list, but the financials are not as good as they were when it was put on the list. We are holding it, but we would not buy any more.
March 3, 2011

If you have been concerned about the up and down direction of the market and concerned about the problems of the world that make the market go down, then please keep in mind that the signal for a downturn is 1250 on the S and P 500. We are a long way from that, so it is best to stay with stocks.

However, we are approaching May which is a time to sell stocks and accumulate cash for buying bargains after the downturn. Starting around April 15th, we will begin to sell one or

two positions a day until we are mostly in cash. For more information on this strategy, see our article Change of Season.
February 26, 2011

BMB Munai (KAZ) is being acquired. There is a payment of aproximately $1.07 per share that will be sent to stockholders in about six months. We have decided to sell and go on to something else.
February 1, 2011

We have made no changes to the Strong Buy List for February. We still believe that there will be a moderate bull market for the next two months, so we will remain fully invested.

January 17, 2011

The media is full of Outlooks for 2011. The good news is that there is a recovery underway and if it gains momentum it could be a very good year for stocks. The bad news is that there is a huge debt in the nations, the states, the counties, and the cities and that could interfere with the recovery. Watch for interest rates and if they go up it is time to cut back on stock investment.

Although it is a short time we have been in 2011, there is data from Dow Jones on asset performance. In the first 15 days, Tech Stocks outperformed all other assets. This includes gold, silver, corn, wheat, real estate, bonds, emerging market stock, everything measured by Dow Jones. If this changes, we will post it in the Journal. In the meantime, we are going to look for some more Strong Buy Tech Stocks.
January 1, 2011

Here are the results for 2010:

DOW   up 11%
S and P 500 up 13%
NASDAQ   up 17%

Strong Buys 2011
2011
Agriculture

Name	Ticker	Price	Target
Chiquita	CQB	8.34	15.00
Zhonqpin	HOGS	7.60	25.00
Coffee Holding	JVA	7.49	12.00
Archer-Daniels	ADM	24.81	33.00

Energy

NF Energy	NFEC	5.20	12.00
PostRock Energy	PSTR	5.64	9.00
VAALCO	EGY	4.86	10.00

Financials

QC Holdings	QCCO	4.35	8.00
ING	ING	10.29	17.00

Shipping

DryShips	DRYS	4.81	10.00
Safe Bulkers	SB	7.91	18.00
Seanergy	SHIP	1.11	2.70
Navios Maritime	NM	5.83	11.00

Technology

CDC Software	CDCS	6.97	12.00
ZST Digital	ZSTN	7.48	17.00

Click on the Ticker for latest price, chart, news and description.
Quotes by www.google.com/finance
Archives of Past Strong Buys

Sold Positions

Name	Ticker	Price Bought	Price Sold
Green Plains	GPRE	9.30	12.18
9/30 Return	$ +2.88	+31%	
Seagate	STX	10.14	14.71
10/29 Return	$ +4.57	+45%	
Stone Energy	SGY	11.31	19.51
11/15 Return	$ +8.20	+73%	
Cosan	CZZ	11.59	13.25

12/28 Return	$ +1.66	+14%	
Micron	MU	7.21	9.71
1/14 Return	$ +2.50	+34%	
BMB Munai	KAZ	.86	1.02
2/25 Return	$ +.16	+19%	
SMART Modular	SMOD	5.96	9.15
5/20 Return	$ +3.19	+54%	
Advance America	AEA	4.03	9.02
7/13 Return	$ +4.99	+124%	

Journal Entries
October 1, 2010

September has been a good month for the market, but the S and P 500 started the year at 1132 and now is about 1141. This is not much gain for nine months. We are still waiting for the last week of October to start buying. Perhaps the November to May market will follow historical patterns, even though September did not.

September 1, 2010

Our new method for buying and selling is now posted. There will be fewer "Strong Buys" but those that make the list will be the "strongest of the Strong Buys". If we sell any of these we will post the "Sold" postion right after the Stong Buy list with a (+ or -) return percentage.

If an investor follows the strong buy list, there will now be a stated exit from the position. In all cases, a stock on the strong buy list should be sold when the target is reached.

August 1, 2010

We have reached 1100 on the S and P 500

index, which may signal an upward move in the market. We will remain active until August 15th and then begin to sell all but the Strong Buy stocks or stocks we are holding for the long term. We will avoid active trading in September and October. For more information about this strategy, see the article, Change of Season.

We are working on a new posting method which will post Strong Buys and when they should be sold. It should be ready in a few months and give higher and safer returns to those that follow our Strong Buy method.
June 1, 2010

We are posting the Strong Buy list for June, but are also advising not to take any new positions until the S and P 500 index reaches 1100, which would signal a new upward trend in the market. There are lots of trading strategies for this type of market, but the only one that works is wait for the upward move.
May 19, 2010

The S and P 500 index has crossed below the 100 day moving average at 1140 and is not far from the 200 day line at 1100. It is time to implement a plan for a market downturn. If you do not have one, feel free to use ours which is at Checklist for a Downturn.

This downturn may only last a few days, or it may last for several months. What ever your plan or method is, "do something". Do not stand by and let the value of your portfolio shrink by 3 to 4 percent per day.
May 1, 2010

Most advisers are saying "Be Careful". The market has been up for over a year. There are many active stocks that are selling at 40 to 50 times earnings. It is a time to be careful, but we do not see any signs of a bear market ahead. It is likely that the market will have much less upside and may even move sideways for a while, making buying the right stocks even more important.

We are changing the Metals and Mining concentration to Technology. There are still a lot of low priced mining stocks that are worth keeping an eye on and we have posted our buying list on the High Risk page, but the regular mining companies have all reached a fair and full valuation. There are no "Strong Buys" in Mining. In the metals area, we still believe that Sutor (SUTR) and General Steel

(GSI) will reach their targets, so there is no reason to sell them, just because we are moving to a Technology concentration.

March 12, 2010

The S and P 500 index (SPY) has been moving up and has reached a 17 month high. We should not have to worry about the direction of the market until June 2010. The index number to watch for is 1110, as this would signal a possible correction.

We are beginning to obtain some twelve month results of our Strong Buy Postings. The results will be at the top of this page from now on. We have stated before that if we post a strong buy, that stock will reach its target price within twelve months. We do not try to forecast further in the future than twelve months.

February 2, 2010

The S and P 500 index (SPY) crossed over the 100 day moving average on January 29, 2010. This is not the end of the market, but it is a time to be more cautious and less speculative. Sometimes the market will move back up almost immediately and the downturn signal will be over. That has happened today and the

index is now around 1099. The number to watch is 1091, which if crossed will signal a downturn. We have posted an article in the Blog area that will outline a method for trading during a downturn.
January 6, 2010

The media is full of "Outlooks for 2010" and the consensus seems to be that investors should make sure they have plenty of developing countries' stocks. We are looking for more stocks from China, Brazil and Australia, but many writers prefer Russia, India and Indonesia.

The P/E for the S and P 500 is now at 25. The historical average is about 15. Stocks are getting overvalued and it is becoming difficult to find Strong Buys in any area. Therefore, we may be adjusting our concentrations in February.

The Federal Reserve has indicated that interest rates will be low throughout 2010. However, if interest rates do start to rise, the best stocks will be in the financial and tech areas.
September 1, 2010

Our new method for buying and selling is now

posted. There will be fewer "Strong Buys" but those that make the list will be the "strongest of the Strong Buys". If we sell any of these we will post the "Sold" position right after the Strong Buy list with a (+ or -) return percentage.

If an investor follows the strong buy list, there will now be a stated exit from the position. In all cases, a stock on the strong buy list should be sold when the target is reached.
...more

November 22, 2009

We are now beginning to obtain some results from the past Strong Buy postings. In the Archives, the results are placed right after the post. There is a summary on the front page.
November 1, 2009

In October, the S P 500 was down for the first time in seven months, but that is traditional since September and October are the down months for the stock market. We have made it to November and by historical data, November to May is the best time to be long in the market. If this year is an exception, remember what Warren Buffet said: "Be fearful when others are greedy, and be greedy when others are fearful."

October 1, 2009

There are no Strong Buys in Mining for October. However, we have noticed that many of the metal processors still meet the criteria of a Strong Buy, so we have added "Metals" to the mining concentration.
August 10, 2009

Teck (TCK) and Gulfport (GPOR) have reached the target price. We have sold all we had and we suggest you do the same. TCK was first posted as a Strong Buy on April 2, 2009 at $6.16 and it is now at $25.43. These are still great companies, but they no longer meet the Strong Buy criteria.

August 10, 2009

It is getting more and more difficult to find Strong Buys in the Mining Concentration. Taseko (TGB) is the only one left that is clearly a Strong Buy. Anglo American (AAUPY) is in a reorganization and changing stock exchanges and the normal evaluation data is not available. We added CDII, which we do believe will double in price, but it gets only about 40% of its revenue from magnesium mining.

We will be adding a Financial Concentration in September to give us more stocks to evaluate.

July 30, 2009

The market has had a nice rally. We should not have to be concerned about a downturn for a while.

July 10, 2009

The market is now at S P 500 877 and is on its way to four weeks of downturn. The 100 day moving average will cross at 860. That is only 17 away. If we reach 860 or lower we will post our method for trading a down market.

5-1-2009

The market is now at S P 500 872 and it seems like some type of recovery is starting. It is also a good time to watch for any sign of a downturn. We use the 100 day moving average of the S P 500 as a signal to quit buying. That crossover right now is at 840. We will post any significant changes.

3-9-09

New Low point. S P 500 676
3-5-09

New Low point. S P 500 682
3-3-09

New Low point. S P 500 696
3-2-09

New Low point. S P 500 700
2-27-09

www.ingramcontent.com/pod-product-compliance
Lightning Source LLC
Chambersburg PA
CBHW071749170526
45167CB00003B/990